SOCIAL STUDIES CONNECT

RIGHTS, RESPONSIBILITIES, AND CONFLICT

SHANTEL GOBIN

Rourke™

BEFORE AND DURING READING ACTIVITIES

Before Reading: *Building Background Knowledge and Vocabulary*

Building background knowledge can help children process new information and build upon what they already know. Before reading a book, it is important to tap into what children already know about the topic. This will help them develop their vocabulary and increase their reading comprehension.

Questions and Activities to Build Background Knowledge:

1. Look at the front cover of the book and read the title. What do you think this book will be about?
2. What do you already know about this topic?
3. Take a book walk and skim the pages. Look at the table of contents, photographs, captions, and bold words. Did these text features give you any information or predictions about what you will read in this book?

Vocabulary: *Vocabulary Is Key to Reading Comprehension*

Use the following directions to prompt a conversation about each word.

- Read the vocabulary words.
- What comes to mind when you see each word?
- What do you think each word means?

> ### Vocabulary Words:
>
> - *citizens*   - *protest*
> - *government*   - *taxes*

During Reading: *Reading for Meaning and Understanding*

To achieve deep comprehension of a book, children are encouraged to use close reading strategies. During reading, it is important to have children stop and make connections. These connections result in deeper analysis and understanding of a book.

 Close Reading a Text

During reading, have children stop and talk about the following:

- Any confusing parts
- Any unknown words
- Text to text, text to self, text to world connections
- The main idea in each chapter or heading

Encourage children to use context clues to determine the meaning of any unknown words. These strategies will help children learn to analyze the text more thoroughly as they read.

When you are finished reading this book, turn to the last page for **After-Reading** activities.

TABLE OF CONTENTS

WE THE PEOPLE

There are more than seven billion people around the world!

We all have to live together and get along with each other.

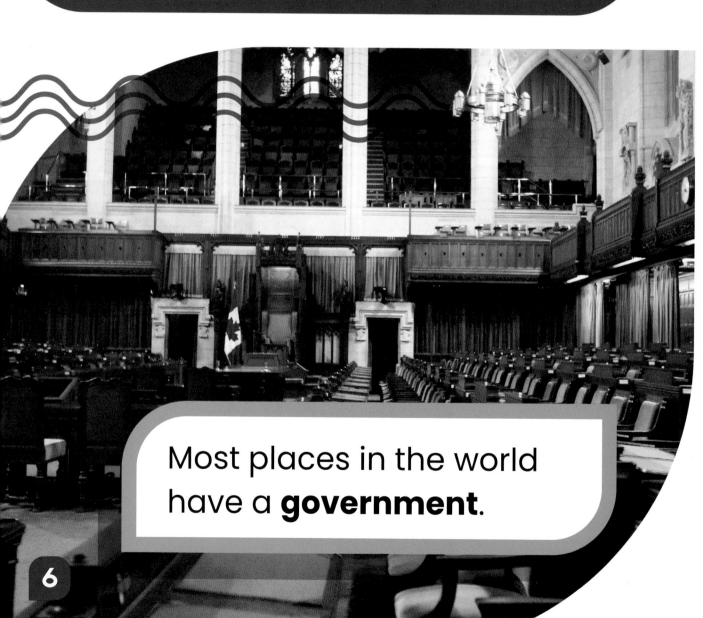

Most places in the world have a **government**.

A government leads the people.

Most governments listen to their **citizens**.

This is how laws are made in many places.

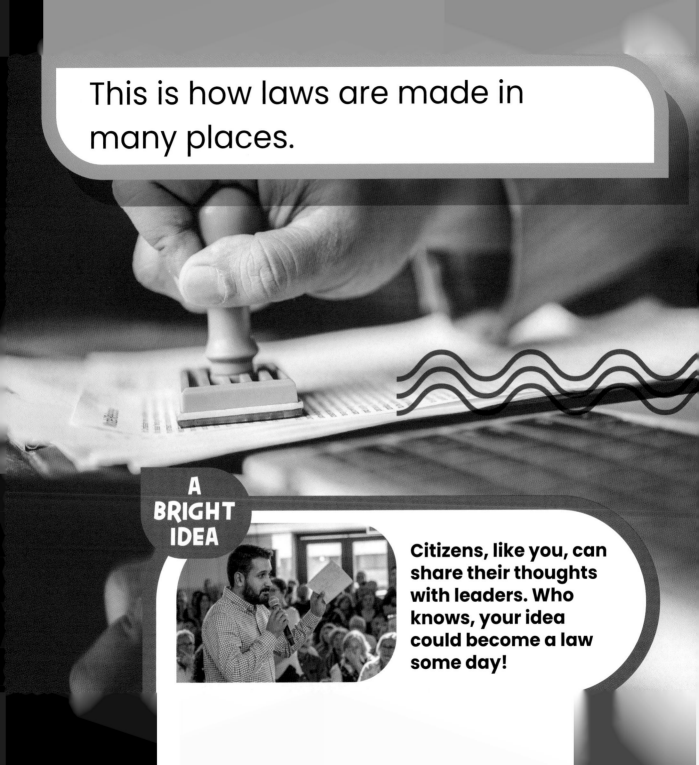

A BRIGHT IDEA

Citizens, like you, can share their thoughts with leaders. Who knows, your idea could become a law some day!

Laws are rules. Some laws help us stay safe.

10

GOOD CITIZENS

A good citizen helps their community.

They pay **taxes** that fund teachers and police officers.

Kids can be good citizens too. They can do things that help their community, or even the whole world!

Xiuhtezcatl Roske-Martinez started protecting our planet at six years old! He travels the world to teach people about climate change.

15

White

Colored

Protect Kids NOT GUNS

Laws are not always fair or good for everyone.

THE RIGHT FIGHT

In the United States, it used to be against the law for Black children to go to school with White children. Leaders made a new law in 1954 to change that.

Change is not always easy.

Sometimes, people **protest** to make their voices heard.

Good citizens keep things moving in the right direction.

Almost 200 countries are part of the United Nations. These global citizens fight for equal rights around the world!

PHOTO GLOSSARY

citizens (SIT-i-zuhn-z): people who have full rights in a particular country

government (GUHV-urn-muhn the system by which a country, state, or city is governed

protest (PRO-test): to object strongly to something

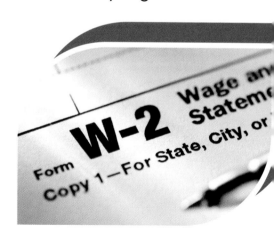

taxes (TAKS-ez): money that people and businesses must pa in order to support a governme

THE GOOD CITIZEN IN ME

Supplies

paper

crayons

How I Can Be a Good Citizen

Directions

1. On your paper, write or draw three ways you can be a good citizen.
2. Ask a friend or family member to do this too.
3. Share your ideas with each other.

Do you have the same ideas? Do you have different ideas? Who do your ideas help?

INDEX

ABOUT THE AUTHOR

Shantel Gobin is an urban educator. She enjoys living in Brooklyn, New York, with her family. She loves being a global citizen and changing the world for the better!

AFTER-READING ACTIVITY

With a parent, go online and do some research. Explore the laws where you live. What are some of the most interesting laws? Are they different or similar to laws in other places around the world? Discuss your research with a family member.

Library of Congress PCN Data

Rights, Responsibilities, and Conflict / Shantel Gobin
(Social Studies Connect)
ISBN 978-1-73165-636-0 (hard cover)(alk. paper)
ISBN 978-1-73165-609-4 (soft cover)
ISBN 978-1-73165-618-6 (eBook)
ISBN 978-1-73165-627-8 (ePub)
Library of Congress Control Number: 2022943016

Rourke Educational Media
Printed in the United States of America
01-0372311937

© 2023 Rourke Educational Media

www.rourkebooks.com

Edited by: Catherine Malaski
Cover design by: Morgan Burnside
Interior design by: Morgan Burnside

Photo Credits: Cover, page 1: ©SDI Productions/ Getty Images, ©FG Trade/ Getty Images, ©PeopleImages/ Getty Images, ©Don Serhio/ Shutterstock.com; pages 4-5: ©metamorworks/ Getty Ir page 4: ©Prostock-Studio/ Shutterstock.com; page 5: ©FatCamera/ Getty Images; page 6: ©bukharo Getty Images; page 7: ©piranka/ Getty Images, ©mathess/ Getty Images; page 8: ©SDI Productions/ Getty Images; page 9: ©Chokniti-Studio/ Shutterstock.com, ©MF_Orleans/ Shutterstock.com; pages 10-11: ©Prostock-studio/ Shutterstock.com; page 11: ©Jeff Baumgart/ Shutterstock.com, ©New Africa Shutterstock.com; page 12: ©SolStock/ Getty Images; page 13: ©Nic Neufeld/ Shutterstock.com; pag 14-15: ©SolStock/ Getty Images; page 15: ©Sipa USA via AP; page 16: ©RonTech2000/ Getty Image ©Heidi Besen/ Shutterstock.com; page 17: ©FatCamera/ Getty Images, U.S. Department of Justice; p 18: ©FilippoBacci/ Getty Images; page 19: ©E4C/ Getty Images, ©DisobeyArt/ Getty Images; pages 2 ©RoterPanther/ Getty Images; page 21: ©gorodenkoff/ Getty Images, ©Entienou/ Getty Images; page 22: ©SDI Productions/ Getty Images, ©NicolasMcComber/ Getty Images, ©FilippoBacci/ Getty Image ©serggn/ Getty Images